Matías Romero, Walter S. Logan

A Mexican Law Suit

An address delivered before the Department of jurisprudence of the

American social science association, at Saratoga, September 5, 1895

Matías Romero, Walter S. Logan

A Mexican Law Suit
An address delivered before the Department of jurisprudence of the American social science association, at Saratoga, September 5, 1895

ISBN/EAN: 9783337313227

Printed in Europe, USA, Canada, Australia, Japan

Cover: Foto ©Suzi / pixelio.de

More available books at **www.hansebooks.com**

A MEXICAN LAW SUIT.

AN ADDRESS

DELIVERED BEFORE THE

DEPARTMENT OF JURISPRUDENCE

OF THE

AMERICAN SOCIAL SCIENCE ASSOCIATION,

AT SARATOGA, SEPTEMBER 5, 1895,

BY

WALTER S. LOGAN,

FOLLOWED BY REMARKS BY

HON. MATIAS ROMERO,

MEXICAN MINISTER TO THE UNITED STATES.

BROOKLYN:
EAGLE BOOK AND JOB PRINTING DEPARTMENT.
1895.

A MEXICAN LAW SUIT.

A Paper Read Before the Department of Jurisprudence of the American Social Science Association, at Saratoga, Thursday Evening, September 5, 1895,

BY

WALTER S. LOGAN.

Saxon jurisprudence had its origin in the anarchy of the German forest ; Latin jurisprudence in the despotism of the Roman Empire. The old Teuton was an untamed freeman ; the Roman, a well-fed, well-ordered, highly developed, and thoroughly disciplined slave. The one demanded justice from his equal as a right, and was ever ready to fight with his own strong right arm for his cause ; the other begged for justice or for mercy from a superior as a boon, and took thankfully whatever was graciously conceded to him.

This distinction survives the time of the Wager of Battle and of the arbitrary decree of a despotic judge. The Common Law Declaration, the Saxon's formulation of his claim, is still the assertion of a right, and concludes with a demand. The Bill in Equity, the typical Latin plea, is now, as it ever was, a petition, and ends with a prayer. The Saxon issue is sharp, clear, concise. It has a clear affirmative and a plain negative—something that you can fight about. The Roman pleadings are long, complicated, verbose. They disclose much to talk about, but little to fight over. The conduct of a modern Saxon suit is after the manner of orderly and civilized warfare. The Latin litigation is, as it ever has been, a persistent plea for grace. The Saxon Jury is an umpire empowered to decide a particular dispute within narrow lines and upon well-established principles. The Latin Judge is the dispenser of a favor or the almoner of a bounty, and is clothed with unbounded discretion. The Saxon Trial is a battle, with the advocate for a commander, and the client, it may be, a candidate for slaughter. Latin legal practice has nothing whatever in it that is at all the equivalent or the counterpart of the Saxon Trial. A Saxon suitor asks only a proper forum and a fair field—a chance to *try.* The Latin suitor ever hides beneath the protecting ægis of the judicial authority. He himself does not *try.* The Saxon Code, where there is one—and the true Saxon is always shy of codes—is but the formulation and crystalization of general rules of law or practice, the result of long previous experience. The Latin Code—and the law in all Latin countries is codified—is the decree of a sovereign power, prescribing most minute and complicated rules of life and conduct.

Latin jurisprudence is in its nature, its essence, and its form, paternal. Saxon jurisprudence, unadulterated, has no trace of paternalism in it.

In England and the United States we have, to some extent, imported Roman law into a Saxon community and grafted the Latin bud upon a Saxon stock.

In Mexico, they have preserved the Latin nomenclature but adopted the substance of a pure Saxon constitution. While, therefore, in form, the Mexican jurisprudence is Latin, in substance it is, in many respects, coming to be even more Saxon than ours.

To trace the reasons for this, it is necessary to go back to pre-European America.

The Indian, like the Saxon, was born for freedom. The wild breezes of his native hills were scarcely more impatient of restraint than was he who was born and dwelt among them. Their chiefs were but chosen leaders, and their government was wont to try rather to direct than suppress the wildness and ferocity of their passions. The forests of aboriginal America and of ancient Germany were, alike, the abode of wild and rough, but free and undaunted, men. In neither the Indian nor the German was there good raw material for a slave.

First and foremost of the inhabitants of aboriginal America, in development, culture and civilization, as well as in all the peculiar racial characteristics of the Indian, stood the Aztec, and other Nahua tribes, of the plateau of central Mexico. They had developed for themselves an orderly government, and wise and well-rooted institutions. They had individual ownership of property, and a complete system of conveyances. They had written laws, courts with well-defined jurisdiction ; and a criminal code, severe, but well adapted to the necessities of their situation. Their government in form resembled a monarchy, but, in reality, it was rather a government of the people in somewhat the same sense as is the English government to-day. It was necessary to have royal blood in order to be eligible to the throne, but the selection from the class possessing the requisite qualifications was made by the representatives of the people, and no monarch was allowed to commence his reign, even after his election, till he had put his courage to the test and shown conspicuous merit upon the field of battle. Around the throne was ever a council, representative of the people and independent of the will of the monarch. The last Montezuma had, it is true, surrounded himself by many of the indicia and accessories of despotic power ; but his life election and all the bulwarks he had erected around his throne could not save him from being removed, and did not prevent the actual substitution of a successor in his place when in the crucial moment he showed the craven spirit and demonstrated his unworthiness for the high place to which he had been elevated.

These Nahua races had never quite discovered the alphabet, but they had devised a system of hieroglyphics that bore a striking resemblance to it and gave them many of the advantages of a written language and a literature. They had no ships upon the sea, nor beasts of burden upon the land ; but, notwithstanding this, they had developed an extensive system of commerce with distant tribes and they had merchant princes, honored there as nowhere else in the world. They had not learned the use of iron, but they shaved themselves with razors made of stone. They used copper and bronze in many of their arts, and excelled even the people of the Old World as workers of gold and

silver. Their civilization was degraded by the practice of human sacrifice, but I do not know that the honorable death upon the temple top
as the chosen victim of the gods, which the Spaniards abolished, was
worse than the horrors of the Auto de Fé, which they introduced. No
man, at any rate, was ever killed in the land of the Aztecs for what he
thought, till the Europeans came and taught them to do it. They had
slavery, but the condition of the slave in Aztec land was far better than
it was in Europe, and his children were free. In all aboriginal America,
no man was ever born a slave.

It was upon the horizon of such a social and political organization
that the Spaniards, with the alphabet, gunpowder, beasts of burden and
European discipline and civilization, appeared.

The Indian was dazed. What he saw was not only new but beyond
his power of comprehension. After a fitful and ill-organized resistance
at first, he was wont to submit. His mental faculties were paralyzed,
and he accepted the new order of things as the decree of inevitable
fate. For three centuries Mexico was ruled entirely by the Latin race.
The language, the habits, the religion and the institutions of the people
became Latinized. There was no longer freedom, even in the barren-
ness of her deserts or the wildness of her forests. The habit of self-
reliance was lost, and people came to look to the powers above them
for guidance, and without questioning to submit their wills to those of
others. Paternalism in State and Church reigned supreme.

Meanwhile, a new race was growing up to take its place among the
peoples of the earth.

Montezuma had in his coffers vast stores of gold, and in his palace
the most beautiful women of all Tenochtitlan. The first thing the
Spaniards did was to appropriate the gold ; the next, to take the women ;
and the foundation of the present Mexican race was laid.

Few women ever came from Spain to Mexico to stay. Few men
came who did not form some sort of connection, lawful or otherwise—
and to their credit be it said it was usually lawful—with some Indian
woman. It was the bravest, the most manly, and the best of the Spaniards who came. There was no place for cowards or sluggards in the
new world. They were popular with the other sex and had their choice

of the women. The Indian maiden preferred even a common Spanish soldier to an Indian king; and so it was the most beautiful, the most accomplished and the best of the Nahua women who became the mothers of the new race.

The reason why the pure Indian degenerated after the European conquest, or, at the most, only held his own, was that his best blood, through his fairest daughters, was beginning to course in Creole veins, and the reason why the Spaniards as a race never gained such a foothold in Mexico as the English did in the colonies north, or as they themselves did in the more southern colonies, was because their racial characteristics were ever being modified and lost or merged in the union of blood out of which the new race was growing.

Nowhere else in America has the aboriginal blood been preserved and the Indian racial characteristics been perpetuated as in Mexico.

The pure aborigine was of a stolid and immobile race. He had not the generations of culture which enables the European to adapt himself to any climate and all conditions ; he had not the mobility which gives the negro the power to survive and multiply alike in frozen Canada or equatorial Africa, as a slave under the lash on the plantations of Cuba and as a freeman under the benign influence of the Stars and Stripes and the Thirteenth Amendment.

Truly did Francis Parkman say of this child of the American forest :

"The Indian is like a rock. You can rarely change the form without destruction of the substance."

The blessings of European civilization were not for the unmixed natives. In the farther South, the Indian tribes were usually too low to attract the white man, and in the far North, in what is now the United States and Canada, the product of the occasional union of the Englishman and Frenchman with the Indian, was simply Indian. The half-breed of either of these races seemed generally to combine only the aggregate vices of his ancestors.

But in Mexico, the Aztec maiden was well worthy of her Spanish lord. She was usually taken for a wife, and always honored as a wife, and so she became the mother of a race and a nation.

We come now to 1800. Three centuries have passed. The new race has multiplied and prospered. It numbers 5,000,000 souls. New race characteristics differing radically from those of either Spaniard or Indian have been acquired and Mexico and the Mexicans are about to take their place among the nations and the races of the earth. It has been three centuries of Latin domination. For three hundred years Spain and the Spaniards have ruled the new land. The Indian had the stolid indifference of age. The Mexican, as a race, was acquiring his growth, developing his character and learning his first racial lessons. Indian and Mexican alike submitted unquestioningly to the Spaniard. No man, unless of pure Spanish blood and born in Spain, was allowed to hold office of trust or emolument in Spanish-America. Birth in Mexico, even of pure Spanish ancestry, was a disgrace, and even parents taunted their children with their inferiority because born in the New World ; so jealous was Spain and the Spaniards of their race and their rule.

It is 1810. The new race is growing and learning. Foreign books are denied them. Foreign teachers are kept away, and foreign ideas prohibited. The ruling Spaniard would sooner introduce a viper into his parlor than a foreign suggestion into a Spanish colony.

But, nevertheless, foreign ideas came, germinated and grew. Down through Louisiana and Texas kept coming the news that a people in the north had raised the glad cry of freedom and independence, and won a glorious victory over European oppression, and that an earnest, thoughtful and self-reliant nation, the architects and the artisans of their own destiny, were prospering as no other nation ever prospered before, with liberty of thought and action as the corner-stone of their new republic. Across the ocean came the news of the French revolution—the revolt of nature against centuries of wrong. French and English books were smuggled in and read even though the terrors of the Inquisition were threatened against any one in whose hands they were found. Even Spain, whose bigotry had hitherto been as stern and unyielding as the rocks of that Gibraltar that England had wrested from her, was beginning to think that she might herself enjoy a little of that liberty which she would not then or ever consent that Mexico should even know about. For a few months, the astonished world was permitted to gaze upon the strange spectacle of the existence of something they called a republic in the land of Philip II, and the news even of this came to Mexico.

And so the Mexican revolution came.

It has sometimes been compared with the American revolution, but there is really no comparison between the two. Ours was the movement of a country for independence ; theirs, the struggle of a people for existence. We sought to give birth to a nation ; they, to baptize a race. We fought for a trifling change of constitution ; they, for the right, theretofore always denied them, to establish institutions. Ours was a struggle of Englishman against Englishman, a child against its unnatural mother ; theirs, a war of races. The Englishman in the colonies had more freedom even than in England, and, having brought his Saxon institutions with him, he had only to maintain them. The Mexican had yet the very alphabet of freedom to learn, and he had to build his institutions new from the foundation stone.

In 1821 the army of the " Three Guaranties," with the dashing and gallant Augustin Iturbide, and that old hero of heroes, Vicente Guerrero, at their head, entered the Mexican capital, and Mexico had won her independence. .But she had gained only the right to learn how to establish her freedom, and half a century more was yet to roll over her head before she obtained established institutions and was able to maintain a well-ordered government.

Full of interest and pathos those fifty years ! The student, the statesman, the philosopher, the patriot, the man who loves his species and hopes for a better civilization and a higher life for mankind, may well dwell upon this period and study intently the struggles of this new race.

For thirty years and more, Mexico was still a Latin country. She early adopted a constitution, in form modeled somewhat after ours. It provided for a federal republic with a president, two houses of congress, a supreme court, and a division of sovereignty between the nation and the state very much such as we have.

But constitutions do not make states. There is a supposed place said to be paved with good resolutions, and history is full of schemes of government promising enough on paper, but in fact impracticable or bad. Here was a people brought up under the most jealous of despotisms, suddenly finding themselves free. As a blind man suddenly restored to sight plunges in the light to which he is unaccustomed even worse than in the darkness with which he has become familiar, so will a people unused to freedom make most unfortunate mis-steps and receive painful wounds before they learn to order their lives, restrain their emotions and organize their social and political relations so that freedom will be a blessing.

For thirty years, Latin Mexico had all the evils of freedom without its benefits, and all the terrors of despotism without its security. Republic overthrew empire ; constitution succeeded constitution ; and government followed government. Now it was a federal republic, now a centralized military despotism. Occasionally there was a regularly elected president, more often a self-appointed dictator. Congresses came and went ; administrations changed ; pronunciamentos appeared so often that they ceased to attract attention, and one rarely knew when he went to bed at night who would be his ruler in the morning.

In their political relations, in their experience in self-government, in their knowledge of how to build and preserve institutions, the Mexican people were children and the child must have many a fall before he can learn to stand alone.

Their institutions, such as they had, during all this time, were Latin. The Church was really the only stable power, and it was the unmodified and unmodernized Latin Church. The administration of justice. such as they had, was after Latin forms, and their jurisprudence was inherited from the Spanish colonial state and was Latin to the core. The customs, the habits, the manner of life and the modes of thought, the whole form of their civilization, were Latin. It could hardly have been otherwise. Children need the guidance of the paternal hand and a race in its childhood instinctively turns to a paternal government.

We come now to 1853. Mexico, as an independent Latin nation, had started in 1821 with an absolute Church and it ended in 1853 with an absolute State as well. It commenced with Iturbide ; it ended with Santa Ana. They had had the Constitutions of 1824 and 1836 and the Constitutional Convention of 1842. They had had the Siete Leyes and the Bases Organicas. They had had the conscientious civil administration of Guadalupe Victoria, Arista and Herrera. They had had far seeing statesmen such as Gomez, Farias, Rosa and Pedraza. They had had military dictator after military dictator, but all had run their course and now they had Antonio Lopez de Santa Ana alone.

We who are so accustomed to Saxon methods can scarcely understand what a Latin revolution means. Our race has had occasionally to dethrone kings and even to cut off their heads. We have fought for independence and won it upon the dikes of Holland and upon the fields of Bunker Hill, Saratoga and Yorktown. We have set up one government in the place of another and modified and changed our constitutions whenever it has become necessary, but the ordinary life of the community has gone on all the time just the same. It has been an alteration of constitutions but not a destruction of institutions. We have re-clothed our government in new attire, and sometimes manacled its limbs, but there has been no disruption of the living and breathing body. It has been a change of appearance to the world outside and occasionally more or less of a reformation of the relations of society inside, but, nevertheless, the progress of our civilization has been a gradual, persistent growth, sometimes slower and sometimes faster, sometimes in one direction and sometimes in another, but always growing. There has never come a time when we have had to stop and commence over again. We have never had to pull down and re-build, to destroy in order that we might create.

But in Mexico it was entirely different. Prior to their revolution, they had no institutions except an absolute Church and an absolute State. Absolutism was everywhere. There was no opportunity to make their change from absolutism to freedom, from despotism to liberty, gradually. When Iturbide and Guerrero entered the City of Mexico at the head of the triumphant army of the nation, all that had been was swept away and they must commence and build anew from the bottom foundation stone up. The old ship of Latin absolutism was broken in pieces upon the rocks. There was nothing left for them to cling to except the floating planks and rigging, and these could at the best only keep their heads above the water for a little time. They were entirely unfit to be worked into, or become a part of, the new ship of a free State.

And now, in 1853, all her efforts seemed to have failed. The earlier Federal Constitution and the later central constitution had both been discarded. States had become provinces, had asserted their independence, and some of them had won it, and the whole foundations of society and government seemed to have been broken up. In their desperation the people had, with a sort of unorganized unanimity, recalled Santa Ana from exile, and intrusted him with the work of framing a new constitution and scheme of government and had given him absolute power while this was being done ; and Santa Ana, thorough Latin as he was, had abused his trust. With the ostensible purpose of preserving order, he had organized a large army which he used only to crush the liberties of the people. He had incited a counter-revolution which had pronounced against the present adoption of any constitution and had proclaimed him dictator for life, with power to appoint his successor. He had overthrown the state governments and trodden under foot all municipal authority. He had dispersed congress and made his cabinet only the personal instruments of his own will. He had destroyed all political machinery and every vestige of the elective franchise. He set about killing or driving into exile every patriot who opposed his rule. He repudiated the very plan that had elevated him to his position, and, having thrown down the ladder by which he had climbed up, he sought to say, as said the great Louis of France : "I am the State ;" and he had an army of ninety thousand men to enforce his imperial will.

Another year passes away. On the first of March, 1854, a small, but brave and earnest band of patriots, who had escaped the bullet of the executioner and the decree of exile, met at the little town of Ayutla in the south of Mexico, and proclaimed the plan under which the present government of Mexico is organized ; and on the eleventh of the same month the plan, somewhat amended, was re-promulgated from the larger town of Acapulco. The movement spread like wild-fire. The people arose everywhere. The exiles came back and took up arms for their country and for freedom, and old Mexico, Catholic Mexico, absolute Mexico, Latin Mexico, ceased to be. The Spaniards had long before been driven from the country and there were few people in it in whom European blood predominated. The inhabitants were in the main either Indians, or Mexicans with an Indian ancestry. Thenceforward, Mexican civilization was to be developed on other than Latin lines, and for the result, whether good or bad, Latin methods and Latin civilization are no longer responsible.

Go back with me to 1806. In the little hamlet of Gelatao San Pablo, in the mountains of Oaxaca, in a hut of straw, was born an Indian boy. There was no drop of European blood in his veins and scarce any trace of European culture did he inherit from his ancestors. His tribe, the Zapotecs, are not known to have been related to the Nahuas in blood, but they were near neighbors of the Aztecs, inhabitants of the same elevated plateau, and akin to them in the courage of their people and in the degree of their civilization. The Zapotecs had, however, lived in a more inaccessible region, had been able to make a more effectual resistance to the Spaniards, and had had their racial characteristics less affected than had the Nahuas by the European invasion. The Zapotecs of 1806 differed but little from the Zapotecs of 1520. For whatever Benito Juarez did or was, the credit is due neither to Saxon lineage nor Latin influence, but to the pure Indian blood of one of the bravest and best of the Indian tribes of North America.

Young Juarez arrived at the age of twelve years without ever having spoken a word of any language except his ancestral Zapotec. Spanish was as foreign to his ear as is Zapotec to ours. Then, by chance, he had an opportunity to go to school, and no blue-eyed Saxon or dark-haired Latin ever applied himself more assiduously or gained knowledge more rapidly than did this copper-colored son of the wild Oaxacan forest. They set him to studying for the Church, but his logical mind refused to accept either its dogmas or its superstitions, and he chose for himself the liberal and elevating profession of the law.

He had moved to the city of Oaxaca, and while still a youth was elected a responsible officer of the municipality. Then he was a member of the State Legislature, Secretary of State and Attorney-General of the State government, and several times representative of his state in the National Congress. Still later, he was repeatedly chosen governor of the state, and so successful were his administrations that while all was anarchy and discord and revolution in the other parts of the Republic, the State of Oaxaca—the Massachusetts of Mexico—was all the time growing and prospering under an orderly and peaceful government, and life and property were as safe there as anywhere in the world.

When Santa Ana became dictator in 1853 and attempted permanently to subvert the liberties of his country and make himself its absolute despot, to the honor of Benito Juarez be it said that he was chosen one of the first victims. Santa Ana had a keen scent for the stalwart foes of despotism. Juarez was thrown into a dungeon at Vera Cruz, and afterwards, as an exile, lived two years in the United States. He was poor and had to earn his own livelihood, and it is said that he did it as a cigar-maker in New Orleans ; but, whatever his hands may have been doing, his mind was ever active and alert for his country's interests and the cause of human freedom. He was all the time studying the Saxon institutions of the United States and qualifying himself for the great part he was to play in the regeneration of Mexico. The moment he heard the call of freedom from Ayutla he started back for his native land, soon found himself the leader of his people, and for twenty years—the twenty years most critical in Mexican history, the twenty years during which the race emerged from childhood into the full vigor of manhood, the twenty years during which it won its freedom, developed its character and established its institutions—this Zapotec Indian from Oaxaca was the faithful and trusted leader of the Mexican nation and the Mexican people.

Fortunate was it for Mexico that this leader was a lawyer rather than a soldier.

We Saxons owe much to our great generals and our soldier-statesmen. They have done noble work for freedom and humanity, but theirs has not been the most important work. The foundation stones of our free

Saxon institutions have been laid by the members of the profession of the law, and the structure of Angelican and American liberty has been reared by lawyers.

Juarez, though born in these mountains of the South, the scene of Mexico's most severe and desperate struggles in all the Indian Wars and the great War of Independence, though he passed his boyhood there during all those years between the defeat of Hidalgo and the triumph of Iturbide, though he lived in a land where the soldier alone seemed to have rank and influence and power and where the military profession was favored above all others, and though he belonged to a race of such valiant fighters that they, almost alone in all Mexico, had been able to persistently resist the power of Spain, yet he himself never bore arms.

It was not because he was not brave. He always displayed the most sublime courage in the time of danger and never flinched in the most desperate of crises. Few men have faced death oftener or with sublimer indifference to personal fate than he. It was not because he lacked the qualities of a great commander. In all those troublous times, he was the coolest and most self-reliant man in the nation, ever ready to strike a telling blow for his country and his cause when the occasion permitted, and equally ready to do that still harder thing— wait for the opportunity when he could best serve by waiting.

It was only because his broad view and clear vision early saw that if Mexico was to be saved and the cause of freedom to triumph there, it must be the work of the lawyer and the statesman, rather than the man of arms.

In 1855, Juarez came back from his exile and commenced the work of de-Latinizing Mexico. The Indian boy of Oaxaca had been among the first to see that free institutions must be built on some other foundations than those on which the structure of despotism in State and Church, through twenty centuries, had been so carefully reared and developed.

And now we come to the most trenchant and far-reaching social and political revolution that the world has ever seen.

Other nations have often substituted one dynasty for another, and changed their constitutions and forms of government; other nations have curbed the power of despotism and given the people constitutional liberty in the place of absolute rule ; other nations have substituted republic for empire, the will of the people for the fiat of the king.

But in Mexico, the revolution went far deeper than all this. It was a change in the very structure of society—even in the relations which neighbor bore to neighbor, husband to wife, and parent to child ; a change in their hopes and in their aspirations ; in everything that pertains to life and to living. When complete, it will be in deed and in truth not only a reorganized and regenerated, but a new and entirely different Mexico. There will be the same old lofty mountains, broad tablelands and fertile valleys, but they will be inhabited by a freer and happier people blessed with a far higher civilization and infinitely more benignant institutions.

That all this must be, Juarez, the Indian boy of Oaxaca, the prophet of his race and nation, saw when he came back from New Orleans and silently took the hands of his companions in hope and danger at Acapulco in 1855.

The first step was the law to which history has given the name of its author. It is called the Ley Juarez.

Half the property in Mexico was owned by the Church. The Church could not be sued, even in an action of trespass or ejectment, except in its own priestly tribunals, and it could sue any citizen for any cause of action in the same tribunal. Litigation in the Church, in reference to Church property, was, therefore, a one-sided affair. The Church sat in judgment in its own case and, it is needless to say, always won.

Half the adult, able-bodied men in Mexico were soldiers, and the army, like the Church, had its own tribunals, not limited, as by our military law, to the punishment of military offences, but giving special protection to the soldier in all his relations in life. Only a soldier sat in judgment between soldier and citizen. Class feeling ran high and the soldier, too, always won.

Juarez had been born among an Indian tribe where there was always equality of rights. He was just back from exile in a land where

equality before the law was the foundation stone of their constitution.
He was himself a careful student of the principles of jurisprudence, and
privileges like these permitted to the Church and the army he knew to
be subversive of all law.

The Ley Juarez abolished all such tribunals, and made every man,
priest, soldier or citizen, amenable to the law of the land and equal in
its courts.

Instantly the Church took up the gauntlet, and turned all its bat-
teries, all the terrors it could pronounce in this world and the next,
against the Ley Juarez and its supporters, and from the promulgation of
this law until the consummation at Queretaro in 1867, the battle cry of
the reactionist party was " Religion y Fueros"—" The Church and the
Privileges." It was truly a battle between liberty and oppression, law
and anarchy, right and wrong.

Equality before the law is the fundamental principle of Saxon jurisprudence, and the final triumph at the Cerro de las Campanas was the
triumph of Saxon liberty over Latin oppression.

But I am twelve years ahead of my story. Twelve most fateful
years were to intervene between the beginning and the end, between the
Ley Juarez and the Hill of the Bells.

The Ley Juarez was followed by the Ley Lerdo, named after Don
Miguel Lerdo de Tejada, Secretary of the Treasury at the time of its
promulgation. Not only did the Church hold half the property of the
nation in its hand, but it was a dead hand. It took but never gave. It
acquired in whatever way it could, even by purchase, if driven to the
dread necessity of payment, but it never sold. Property, when once it
reached the possession of the Church, might as well, so far as the purposes
of trade, development and improvement were concerned, have been wiped
out of existence.

Half the people of the nation were the forced tenants of a Church
which owned allegiance only to a pope five thousand miles away across
the ocean.

The Ley Lerdo allowed the tenants to purchase at a fair valuation
fixed by law and calculated upon its rentals. A few years later, during
the presidency of Juarez, the Ley Lerdo was supplemented by a law

3

nationalizing all Church property and authorizing its sale for the benefit of the people.

Some have called this robbery. I call it restitution. It gave to the people only what they themselves, by three centuries of grinding toil, had fairly earned.

Then came the Constitution of 1857, which, with its later amendments, is the fundamental law of Mexico to-day.

Almost every line of this Constitution shows that the Saxon idea was uppermost in the minds of its authors.

It is more Saxon than ours, and is the most liberal and advanced, and I think the best, written constitution in the world.

Article I declares that :

" The Mexican people recognize that the rights of man are the basis and the object of social institutions."

Of Article II, I give a literal translation :

" In the republic all are born free. Slaves who set foot upon the national territory recover, by that act alone, their liberty, and have a right to the protection of the laws."

This was not a new provision in Mexican Constitutions, being copied from earlier instruments, but even this was two years before Harper's Ferry, six years before the Emancipation Proclamation, and nearly ten years before our Thirteenth Amendment. The Indian boy of Oaxaca certainly antedates John Brown and Abraham Lincoln.

Article III provides that instruction in Mexico shall be forever free. It is now forty years since Ayutla, and we, the great, liberal, free United States, have not entirely learned *this* lesson yet.

Articles IV and V provide that every man may adopt and follow whatever honest calling or occupation he chooses, and that no one shall be obliged to give personal service without compensation and without his full consent.

" The State," says Article V, "shall not permit any contract, pact or agreement, to be carried into effect, which has for its object the diminution, loss, or irrevocable sacrifice of the liberty of man, whether it be for the sake of labor, education, or a religious vow. The law, consequently, may not recognize monastic orders, nor may it permit their establishment, whatever may be the denomination or object with which they claim to be formed."

By a later amendment, the necessity of religious oaths is abolished, marriage is made a civil contract, the State and Church are declared to be absolutely independent, and Congress is not allowed to pass laws " establishing or prohibiting any religion." Every lover of free institutions may rejoice that these are no idle words, and that in fact, as well as in theory, there is absolute, practical religious liberty all over Mexico to-day.

Articles VI and VII give Mexico a free press, and declare that "the liberty to write and publish writings on any subject whatsoever is inviolable."

Not only is the right of petition declared to be inviolable, but every respectful petition addressed to the powers that be must have a respectful answer returned to it. No petition in Mexico can be pigeon-holed and ignored.

The right of public agitation and organization is amply protected by Article IX.

Every man has a right to possess and carry arms, and to enter and go out of the republic, travel through its territory and change his residence, "without the necessity of a letter of security, passport, safe conduct, or other similar requisite."

No hereditary honors, titles of nobility, or prerogatives are permitted.

The Ley Juarez is imbedded in the Constitution in the following words :

"In the Mexican Republic no one may be judged by special law nor by special tribunals. No person or corporation may have privileges or enjoy emoluments which are not compensation for a public service and established by law."

Article XIV reads :

"No retroactive law shall be enacted. No man may be judged or sentenced, except by laws made prior to the act and exactly applicable to it, *and by a tribunal which shall have been previously established by law.*"

This is broader than the similar provision in our Constitution.

Another section provides that,

"No one may be molested in his person, family, domicile, papers and possessions, except in virtue of an order written by the competent authority which shall establish and assign the legal cause for the proceedings."

In Mexico, a man's house is, under the Constitution, as much his castle as in any Saxon country in the world. There can be imprisonment for crimes only. Arrest for debt of any kind is prohibited, nor can a prisoner be detained for the non-payment of a simple fine. The prisons of Mexico are intended for rich as well as poor wrong-doers, and for wrong-doers only, and there is no provision in their law that payment may take the place of punishment.

There can be no detention of a prisoner for any cause beyond the term of three days without "a writ showing cause of imprisonment and other requisites which the law establishes," and " the mere lapse of this term shall render responsible the authority that orders or consents to it, and the agents, ministers, wardens, or jailers who execute it." In every criminal trial, the accused must be confronted with his accuser and with the witnesses who testify against him, and the grounds of the accusation, with full data relating thereto, must appear in the process against him and be fully made known to him. He is entitled to be heard in defence by himself, or by counsel, or by both, and in case he is not able to pay counsel, he may himself select any lawyer in the republic, who must serve him faithfully without compensation.

They do not allow, as we sometimes do, young and inexperienced advocates to experiment on a poor prisoner.

Extraordinary punishments are prohibited as with us.

The post-office is inviolate. It ought to be so here. Better occasionally let a criminal escape than allow, as we sometimes do, Mulberry street detectives to invade the sanctity of private correspondence.

Private property cannot be appropriated except for public use and with *previous* full indemnification. If elevated railroads are built in the City of Mexico, they will have to pay their damages before they commence running their trains instead of a quarter of a century afterwards as in the City of New York.

No municipal or ecclesiastical corporation, "whatever may be its character, denomination or object," has legal capacity " to acquire in proprietorship or administer for itself real estate, with the single exception of edifices destined immediately and directly to the service and object of the institutions."

Monopolies of all kinds are prohibited. Mexico has not yet reached that high state of civilization under which trusts can flourish as they do with us.

The privilege of Mexican citizenship is extended not only to those who are born within the republic or become naturalized as with us, but to every parent of a Mexican child and to every man who owns an acre of land in the republic, no matter where he may reside.

Article L out-Saxonizes the Saxon. It reads :

"The supreme power of the federation is divided for its exercise into legislative, executive and judicial. Two or more of these powers shall *never be united in one person or corporation* nor the legislative power be deposited in one individual."

The law-making power is vested exclusively in the congress of the republic, which consists of two chambers, and a simple majority of each body can enact a law over the president's veto.

There is a division of sovereignty between the Nation and the States similar to that provided for in our constitution.

The federal judiciary consists of a supreme court and circuit and district courts, with powers similar to those of our federal judiciary, and the state courts throughout the republic are generally organized very much as our state courts are, and with similar jurisdiction.

It will be seen that this constitution is patterned a good deal after ours, and that wherever there has been a departure from the precedent we set, it has been in the direction of more liberal provisions and more stringent guarantees of individual liberty and private property. We can well imagine it to be such a constitution as our forefathers would have framed if our constitutional convention had sat in 1857 instead of 1787.

If you judge the two constitutions—theirs and ours—by their simple intrinsic merits, Mexico would have no reason to fear the result of the judgment.

But if you consider the circumstances under which the two constitutions were framed, Mexico may well indeed be proud of what was done for her by the patriots of Ayutla.

In our Constitutional Convention sat some of the wisest and most learned statesmen of all the world, men who had learned their statesmanship not so much in books as in the practical administration of affairs in their own states and in the Continental Congress. They came of a race of men who had been accustomed to govern themselves for centuries back ; a race which had been educated in the town meeting, and had acquired self-reliance in the hard school of Saxon liberty. They had before them the writings of all the great philosophers and thinkers of Europe ; and they sat in a time of profound peace, years after the country had securely won its independence, and when they could deliberate with perfect leisure.

The Mexican Constituent Congress was composed of men belonging to a race which had little history behind it and no experience in self-government. They were providing a constitution for a people who had known only three centuries of absolutism and thirty years of anarchy, and as they sat in their convention hall the cannon of their reactionary enemies boomed on half the hills of Mexico, and they knew that they must lay down their pens to take up their swords. They must fight in battle to establish all that they then resolved in convention.

If they had been wise and learned and experienced Saxons, their work would be entitled to the world's commendation. How much more should we honor them when we remember how utterly without experience and without precedent they were. Our Constitution-makers furnished us with good bricks for the temple of liberty, but they were made with an abundance of straw ; their constitution-makers made just as good bricks out of nothing but stubble.

The partisans of reaction and absolutism—an absolute Church and a Latin State—turned instinctively to the Latin Monarchies of Europe for help and protection against this idea of Saxon liberty which the Mexican people, under the guidance of their wise, brave, and true Indian-lawyer leader, were accepting as the foundation of their hopes and aspirations.

Louis Napoleon had stolen the proudest Latin throne in Europe and he was quite willing to be a party to the larceny of another on this side the ocean, on which a Hapsburg and a relative of Philip II might sit in theory, while he, the nephew of his great uncle, might rule in fact.

And so came the War of the French Invasion, as cruel, as uncalled for, as unjust, as any war in history.

Its avowed object was to overthrow the free Saxon institutions that the Mexican people had chosen for themselves and to restore Latin absolutism in Church and State.

Louis Napoleon, from Fontainebleau, writes General Foréy, about to set out for Vera Cruz, July 3, 1862, that it is not for the interest of France that Saxon institutions, such as they have in the United States, shall be established in Mexico, but that "if a stable government be established there with the assistance of France, *we shall have restored to the Latin race from the other side of the ocean, its strength and prestige* * * and we shall have established our beneficent influence to the center of America."

" Now, therefore," continues this upstart emperor of the Latin race, "our military honor pledged, the exigency of our politics, the interest of our industry and our commerce, make it our duty to march on Mexico, to plant there boldly our standard, *to establish there a monarchy.*"

And it was as Latins, and for the advancement of Latin absolutism, that they set to work to accomplish their fell purpose.

The French emperor had arranged his course of procedure with Almonte, a reactionist exile from Mexico. It had been agreed between the two—the Mexican monarchist and the Latin monarch—that a French army of invasion should land in Mexico and that whatever force was necessary should be used to establish there a monarchy with the perhaps well-meaning, but certainly incapable, and ill-fated Maximilian as emperor of Mexico.

General Foréy, as commander of the French forces, called an assembly of notables, carefully selecting, with Almonte's advice, the men who were to compose it. Naturally, there was not a known republican or a constitutionalist in the assembly.

And they, this so-called assembly of notables, selected by the commander of a foreign army of invasion and conquest, from which every patriot and every lover of freedom was excluded with the most extreme care, went through the form of decreeing as follows :

"*First.* The Mexican nation adopts a monarchial, temperate and hereditary form of government, under a Catholic Prince.

"*Second.* The Sovereign shall take the title of Emperor of Mexico.

"*Third.* The imperial crown of Mexico shall be offered to his Imperial and Royal Highness, Prince Ferdinand Maximilian of Austria, for him and his descendants.

"*Fourth.* In case, from circumstances which cannot be foreseen, the Archduke Ferdinand Maximilian should not take possession of the throne which is offered to him, the Mexican nation shall place it under the consideration of his Majesty, Napoleon III., Emperor of the French, that he may indicate another Catholic Prince to whom the crown shall be offered."

The last paragraph was rendered necessary by the fact that Maximilian—it seems alone of all these conspirators against the peace and freedom of Mexico—had a conscience and might give them trouble. He really would not accept even a throne from the lavish hand of Napoleon unless he was first convinced that he had been elected to it in some way by the Mexican people.

To satisfy him, they had to go back to Mexico and pretend to hold an election, though no election was, in fact, ever held. They simply took over a lot of petitions and doctored returns, and really buncoed this high-minded, but exceedingly gullible, Austrian Prince.

It might be inferred from the language of this decree that some limit was to be imposed upon the power of the monarch, and that it was intended that the country should have some sort of constitution—although Latin sovereigns are not very much given to constitutions unless they are forced upon them—but no constitution ever came, and, while Maximilian ruled, it was with a sway as absolute as that of the Czar of Russia. The infamous decree or statute of the 3d of October, 1865, under which the best blood of Mexico flowed and the stanchest and most devoted patriots of the nation met their death, and which was the just cause of his own execution, was issued by "Maximilian, Emperor of Mexico, our Council of Ministers and our Council of State, with one accord decreeing."

The Council of Ministers and the Council of State referred to were of his own arbitrary selection. In the government of Maximilian the people had no voice whatever.

This bloody statute provided that every patriot taken in battle, or with arms in his hands, or who was a member of any patriotic band or armed gathering, "whether or not they proclaimed a political pretext," and every man who furnished food, clothing or shelter, whether voluntarily or by force, to a patriot band or a patriot soldier, should suffer death within twenty-four hours after capture.

Some of our ancient Saxon ancestors have won and deserved a fierce and bloody name in history, but they were never quite so ferocious or blood-thirsty as these Nineteenth Century Latins in Mexico.

There was a Saxon republic just north of Mexico that was quite occupied with its own affairs at the particular time when Maximilian came over to teach the people of the American continent the science of Latin government, but, one day at Appomattox, they settled up this business of theirs so that then they had more time to devote to his majesty, the Emperor of the French, and by almost the next mail, our great secretary, William H. Seward, wrote to Louis Napoleon that the French soldiers must be withdrawn from Mexico, or our soldiers, just then out of business, would go there too and take a hand in the quarrel ; and so Louis Napoleon went home and Maximilian met his fate at Queretaro on the 19th of July, 1867.

And thus ended Latin absolutism, and thus was established Saxon freedom in the Mexican nation. No Latin prince has since shown any eagerness to follow in Maximilian's foot-steps.

But no one knew better than the wise and far-seeing statesmen who were responsible for the Constitution of 1857 that the customs, habits and modes of thought of a people cannot be changed by the formal adoption of a new constitution.

It takes an hour, or a day, or a month to enact a law ; it takes generations to establish institutions. A people whose ancestors for hundreds of years have been educated in Latin absolutism cannot become fully developed Saxon freemen all at once. The Mexican statesmen of 1857 saw this then quite as clearly as we see it now, and in nothing is their wisdom and foresight better shown than in the fact that they were careful not to attempt too much at once. They had, indeed, laid the corner-stones of their free institutions on a broad, secure and enduring foundation, but the superstructure they left for time and the system of

4

free education they so carefully provided for, to complete. And so Mexico continued really Latin in form, though in reality her institutions have been since then much more after the Saxon than the Latin idea.

But we are concerned to-night with jurisprudence, and the jurisprudence of a nation is the supreme test of the practical excellence of its civilization. That people has made the most progress that knows best how to try a law suit. The provision of a proper forum in which private controversies may be settled is the most important sphere of government. On the proper and actual administration of justice between man and man depends more than on anything else the degree of a nation's prosperity and the happiness of its people.

A law suit in Mexico furnishes, perhaps, the best illustration of the union of Latin forms with Saxon realities. I have already shown how in criminal trials, the substantial rights guaranteed by our Saxon Magna Charta are imbedded in the Mexican constitution. The accused is confronted with the accusation, the accuser and the witnesses. He is defended by counsel of his own selection, and even so entirely Saxon an institution as trial by jury has won its way into this as well as other countries educated in Latin ideas.

But the Saxon guaranties and the Saxon jury are under the control of a judge who has been educated in Latin forms, acquired his learning from Spanish books, and who is not always fully imbued with the true Saxon spirit, and, moreover, he is apt to be enveloped by an atmosphere from which the old taint has not been altogether removed. The Saxon statute light which is intended to direct his course is still often seen through Latin spectacles, and we must not expect or desire too close an imitation of our favorite methods, nor must we be too sure that the lusty food that suits our northern stomachs and ponderous vital mechanisms is always the best for all people all over the world under all conditions.

The Saxon criminal procedure, especially as administered in the United States, is inclined to be somewhat slow and dilatory. It takes time to wrap around the accused, and very probably guilty, citizen all the guaranties of the Magna Charta and to convict and punish him without doing violence to our inherited ideas of criminal procedure. If you have but a little crime to punish, it is all right; but in a condition of society where offences against the law become for any reason peculiarly prevalent, our system shows at its worst.

The condition of things in Mexico has been such that celerity and certainty of punishment have often been more important than a nice observation of the provisions of the Magna Charta or even of their own most excellent constitution. The civil wars had left the roads full of bandits, the mountains infested with robbers, the streets teeming with highwaymen, and had so confused many people's ideas of *meum* and *tuum*, that portable property was likely to change hands very rapidly, and a cross by the roadside was often the only record left of the resisting owner. Violent diseases may require summary remedies, and Mexico's statesmen saw that Mexico must be cured of the bandit fever at no matter what cost. Fortunately, the bandits usually resisted and were killed while being arrested or while attempting to escape, instead of being saved for more regular execution afterwards ; but even if brought before the magistrate, the bandit was given but short shrift, and conviction followed accusation, and execution conviction, with a celerity which, I fear, left little room for an abstract discussion of the rights of either Englishmen or Mexicans, or of the guaranties of their Constitution or ours, and which is at least not usual in the city of New York where I practice law.

I cannot say that this method was entirely peculiar to Mexico. In states and territories of the American Union similarly situated the people, even the most pronounced of the Saxons, were wont to imitate their brethren on the other side of the line and adopt methods similar to theirs when methods ideally better would not work.

We may, and we do, criticise the methods of enforcing the criminal law which were at one time quite prevalent among our western and southern neighbors, both in Mexico and the United States, and they are doubtless fit subjects for just criticism, but it is due to Mexico that it should be said that in the last twenty-five years—the only twenty-five years she has ever had of real self-government—she has done so much to rid the country of her criminal classes that life and property are as safe there to-day as anywhere in the world ; and it does not become the generation that reaps the benefit to criticise too much the methods of those who did the work.

As the criminal classes have been suppressed, as the country has become quiet, and peace and order have taken the place of the preceding anarchy and war, criminal trials are coming more and more to conform to the true spirit of the Mexican Constitution and the ideas of Saxon freemen, and no one who has watched the progress of events in Mexico since she first began so stand erect and breathe the inspiring air of freedom, can have any doubt as to whither it is tending.

The continuance of Latin forms is even more prevalent and more marked in civil than in criminal cases.

The proceedings to commence a suit are especially peculiar.

There had been imported from Spain in the old colonial days a practice of summoning a proposed defendant first before the Court of Conciliation, presided over by a judge who was *not*, and was not allowed to be, a lawyer, and who heard no evidence, summoned no witnesses, and had no jurisdiction to determine any question in dispute. His duty was simply to see if he could not induce the parties to settle or compromise their differences before they plunged into the vortex of an actual law suit. His good offices were placed at their services whether they sought them or not, and it was only on a certificate from him that the dispute could not be compromised that they were admitted to the ordinary tribunals.

When the republic was established, this practice was continued and there was actually a provision in the Constitution of 1824 that no civil suit could be commenced in a Mexican court until the parties had first been summoned before the Court of Conciliation, and that court had found that the difficulty would admit of no amicable adjustment.

The practice is still continued, though now without the sanction of any constitutional requirement, but it is coming to be more and more only a form. This Court of Conciliation is entirely paternal in its origin and its character, and adapted only to a people accustomed to submit themselves to the kind care of a paternal government. It is a common feature of Latin legal procedure, and now exists in most of the Latin nations of Europe.

We Saxons never had anything of the kind. It is contrary to our ideas and the genius of our institutions. If we wish to compromise a difficulty, we do it as freemen, rely on our own judgment, take the responsibility ourselves, and prefer to make our own compromises without the assistance of an official compromiser.

In its inception, the Court of Conciliation was a most important part of the structure of the government, and was constantly called upon to perform its important function. The fact that it is degenerating now into a form only shows, as perhaps nothing else can, that far-reaching and beneficent Saxon influences are at work in the rising Republic south of the Rio Grande.

In nothing is the difference between their way and ours shown more clearly than in the method of disposing of the issue.

We try it. It was always the Saxon practice to try it. They had somewhat rough and uncouth and unsatisfactory methods of trial in the early days. The cross-examiner, as an institution of the court room, is a product of modern evolution. Before his advent, if one man asserted the affirmative of a proposition of fact and another had a different recollection, they settled the question by challenging one another and fighting it out, and the most skillful fencing master was the one whose story was credited. The substitution of the trained advocate, the learned judge, the impartial jury and modern methods for eliciting and discovering the truth was a long step in advance, but we have still clung to the *trial* as a distinctive and never-to-be-abandoned feature of Saxon self-reliance as applied to the administration of orderly justice.

There comes a time in the history of every Saxon law suit when the plaintiff and the defendant must face one another with their witnesses and their advocates in the forum of justice, and finally submit their differences to the arbitrament there provided.

Under the Latin practice there was nothing at all the equivalent of our trial. From the commencement of the litigation, the judge took entire charge of the case. He summoned the parties and the witnesses before him, one at a time, as suited his convenience, and in the privacy of his own closet they each poured their story into his receptive ear. If he was a peculiarly honest and scrupulous man, he took nothing at these interviews but testimony, but if he was simply an ordinary judge, he took what he could get, and if the case was an important one his opportunities were by no means insignificant. Having gone through the process of hearing the testimony till he was tired of it or until his harvest was all gathered, he, sooner or later—usually later—decided the case. If he was a learned man skilled in the law, he decided it himself ; otherwise—and it was usually otherwise, for the judges were seldom lawyers —he got some one else to decide it for him who knew how better than he.

As neither party had heard the evidence on the other side, no one could dispute the wisdom of the decision.

In Mexico, they retain in form the old Spanish methods of determining an issue of fact. The statement of the parties and the testimony of each witness is taken by the judge in private ; neither party nor witness is confronted with his adversary or with other witnesses, or submitted to the ordeal of an oral cross-examination, and the judge decides the case, when he gets ready, in his own way ; but counsel are allowed to submit questions and cross-questions to the judge, to be propounded by him to the witnesses and the parties, and this is the usual practice. The testimony is all reduced to writing, and when completed submitted to the other side and counsel are heard upon it, usually in writing, but sometimes orally.

Mexican judicature appears here at its worst. No one appreciates the weakness of the system more than the good lawyers—and the country is coming to be full of them—who practice in their courts, and there will doubtless soon be a change for the better. It is beginning to come already in some of the states of the republic, and an oral cross-examination is, in some cases, permitted.

But even now, the practice is infinitely superior to the old Latin system. Publicity, the best of all security against wrong-doing, is secured ; the calcium light of public opinion is turned upon the action of the judge in every case, and if he commits an error the courts of appeal are ready and prompt to give redress.

There is still a good deal of delay, unavoidable to the system, but I do not know that there is any more than there is with us under our better system. It is, at the worst, far better than it ever was before, and in the practical administration of justice there are fewer annoying delays and grievous abuses. In many respects it compares very favorably with the administration of justice in the United States.

In former years it was the exception rather than the rule to select a judge from the bar, but now the lawyers among the judges are getting to be in the great majority, and, so far as my acquaintance goes—and it is quite extended—the judges are usually men of high character and anxious to do equal and exact justice between man and man without fear or favor.

At the time of the adoption of her Constitution, the condition of Mexican society was not such as to make an extensive use of the jury system practicable, but, as the work of education goes on—and it is going on very rapidly ; as the level of public intelligence is raised—and it is being raised very fast; and as the people become more and more accustomed to managing their own affairs and relying upon their own efforts, there will come the material for a jury system, and trial by jury will undoubtedly be generally introduced in civil, as it is already in criminal cases, and with the Saxon jury must go the other concomitants of a Saxon trial.

This is a consummation which the best statesmen, the best patriots, and the best lawyers in Mexico devoutly hope for, and it is pretty sure to come.

The feature of Saxon jurisprudence most important, however, is the independence of the judiciary.

Few people fully appreciate the far-reaching nature of those provisions of our National and State Constitutions dividing government strictly into the executive, legislative and judiciary departments, and prohibiting *ex post facto* laws and laws impairing the obligations of contracts.

The law must be general in its operation ; must precede the offense, and be determined and applied only by permanent and regularly appointed judicial officers, who have neither executive nor legislative powers. There may be *privileges and immunities* without these guaranties, but there can be no *rights*. They are necessary foundation stones in every temple of freedom.

With the Latins all authority over the bodies or the souls of men came from some superior power—King or Pope—and the same authority might enact the law, interpret and determine it, and carry it into execution. If no law or tribunal was found that fitted the case, a new one might be manufactured for the occasion, or an old one re-interpreted to new uses.

The Mexican Constitution of 1857, as we have seen, contains provisions more stringent even than ours for the protection of the independence of the judiciary. It provides that government shall be divided into legislative, executive and judicial departments, and that "two or more of these powers shall never be united in one person or corporation." It forbids forever retroactive laws, and provides " that no man may be judged or sentenced except by laws made prior to the act and exactly applicable to it, *and by a tribunal which shall have previously been established by law,*" and special laws and special tribunals are expressly interdicted.

No words could be more broad and decisive than those used by the makers of the Mexican Constitution in protecting that bulwark of freedom, judicial independence. They knew well their prevailing danger and they guarded against it with all the means at their command. There is no doubt that their action produced an immediate and most beneficial effect, and that Mexico's relief from the evils which had been hanging over her so long began at once.

A true and impartial statement of the case requires, however, two additions to what has already been said upon the subject :

1. The executive power of Mexico down to very recent times has had, and still has, in practice, more influence upon the judiciary than is consistent with the letter and the spirit of these most admirable provisions of the Constitution of the Republic, and the judicial power is not as independent as it ought to be.

2. The influence of the executive over the judicial power is growing less and less every year, and the judiciary are becoming more and more independent The evil yet exists, but it is infinitely less than it was; it is all the time diminishing, and it bids fair soon to disappear altogether.

Let us not complain or criticise too much. When a people are traveling, as the people of Mexico are, with accelerating speed in the right direction, we can well afford to give them time to reach the goal they have so firmly and heroically set for themselves. We must remember that it is scarcely more than a quarter-century since Queretaro.

In the phraseology of deeds and forms of contract still in use in Mexico the paternal theory of jurisprudence is well shown. In ancient Spanish times, when one person wished to make a conveyance to another, the two went before a notary public and stated the whole case to him. The notary inquired into the most minute details of the transaction, investigated the value of the property, passed upon the sufficiency of the consideration, looked into the circumstances of the parties to see if the affair was one which was in every way to the advantage of the parties, and, in general, acted the paternal to the fullest degree. Then finally came the deed. It was not, as with us, a simple instrument signed and acknowledged by the grantor and containing in terse form words of grant, but it was a most prolix and tedious affair. It was in the form of a recital by a notary that the parties had come before him and the one said so and so, and the other said something else, and that he had looked into everything connected with the transaction, questioned their neighbors and investigated their business ; and he tells, with a detail that is sickening if you are in a hurry, as we Saxons always are, all the conclusions to which he arrives, and finally states that the one party says he is willing to convey, and the other to accept, the property ; and the notary, not the parties, signs the deed, with about the same degree of solemnity that a priest would perform the marriage ceremony. Then some magistrate goes out with the parties, walks around the property and fixes its metes and bounds, and it is the magistrate, not the vendor, who actually delivers possession to the purchaser.

Some of these forms are still kept up in Mexico, but as forms only. The notary copies the deed, questions, answers and everything, from a form book, barely changing the necessary details to fit the circumstances, and the parties sign and deliver it just as we do. There is still kept up also the form of exchanging possession in the presence of the magistrate, but this is likewise coming to be mere ceremony. Some day they will enact the most excellent statute we have in New York State for short forms of deeds and their system of prolix conveyancing will be at an end.

In contracts, as in deeds, the magistrate in form plays the old paternal part. The statutes still retain many of the ancient provisions, such as giving a party the right of rescission, etc., if the consideration is not such as to satisfy the mind of the protecting and fatherly magistrate, or if something should happen that had not been thought of, or if there was some other reason which appealed to the Latin conscience ; but all evil results are now avoided and the teeth of paternalism in the transaction effectually drawn by inserting in the contract an express statement, as is now always permissible, that the parties waive the benefit of these well-intentioned, but mischievous and meddlesome, provisions of the law, and choose to stand upon their responsibility, and attend to their own business as freemen.

The spirit of Saxon self-reliance is really spreading in Mexico faster than the casual observer can imagine, and with it are coming stronger and prouder men and better citizens all over the land.

I cannot leave you to-night without saying a word about the members of our profession in the Republic of Mexico.

Upon the advocates of a country, more than upon its judges, depends the administration of its justice. They form the only reservoir from which an able and accomplished judiciary can be drawn ; they form the only background upon which a pure judiciary can be projected; and they make the atmosphere, fair or foul as it may be, which the judiciary must ever breathe.

The Latin judge sat in the silence of his closet. There was no opportunity for the persuasive eloquence of the advocate.

The Saxon judge sits in the forum, where the advocate is at home.

In Latin Mexico there were many men learned in the law, but few lawyers. The advocate was not there. In the first republic, the republic before Ayutla, anarchy rather than law reigned, and arms and not advocacy was the favored profession. The war of the French Intervention occupied men's minds till it was ended at the Hill of the Bells. Then, for the first time, was there a proper field for the advocate in the Mexican nation.

And so the lawyer in Mexico is just beginning to be a power and to make his influence felt.

It is my good fortune to be favored with the personal acquaintance and friendship of many of Mexico's able and accomplished lawyers and advocates, and I can say of them, from my personal knowledge, that their eloquence would delight any audience, and their learning grace any court house in these United States of ours.

SEÑOR ROMERO'S REMARKS.

Mr. Chairman, Ladies and Gentlemen : While I feel very thankful for the honor you have bestowed upon me in inviting me to the present session of the Law Department of the American Social Science Association, given up to Mexican Jurisprudence, I, at the same time, exceedingly regret that in the printed program of this evening's proceedings I appear as making an address after Mr. Logan's paper. I would feel greatly honored to follow our distinguished friend if I had had the time and opportunity to prepare something worthy of this assembly, but the invitation I received came to me too late ; and, besides, I did not understand that it was an invitation to make an address to-night that I had accepted, and, consequently, have made no preparation. You can readily imagine, therefore, my embarrassment when I have to speak in a language that is not my own, after the very able paper we have just heard and before such a distinguished audience as is here present. Instead of making an address or anything which would be worthy of that name, I will only enter into an unceremonious conversation with you on some topics that may be of interest to you, as they are connected with Mexican Jurisprudence, and of which I am reminded by the able paper just read.

But before doing so, I wish to express my admiration for the masterly manner in which our friend, Mr. Logan, has treated the subject of Mexican Jurisprudence, under his chosen title of "A Mexican Law Suit." It is really remarkable that, with the comparatively few opportunities he has had for obtaining practical knowledge of Mexican laws and the habits and usages of the people, he should have mastered his subject in such a wonderful way and have expounded it in the able and comprehensive manner in which he has done here to-night. It is very difficult, as you can all realize, to understand the laws, habits and customs of a foreign country, unless you have been a long-time resident of it and have made a special study of that particular subject, and it is, therefore, surprising that with such scanty facilities as Mr. Logan has had he should have accomplished so much and shown it so clearly as he has here to-night.

There are, however, a few points upon which I would like to dwell, not in criticism of Mr. Logan's paper, because that is unassailable and because it would not be becoming in me to attempt such a criticism, even if there were ground for it, but rather by way of amplification as to some of the different characteristics of the laws of Mexico which he discussed.

In referring to the provision of Article II of our Constitution of 1857, which decreed that "everybody is born free in Mexico and that any slave obtains his liberty by stepping on Mexican soil," Mr. Logan correctly stated that our Constitution made slavery forever unlawful in Mexico five years before Lincoln's famous proclamation which abolished it in the United States, although in fact, the abolition of slavery was accomplished in our country a great many years before. In fact, Hidalgo, the promoter of our independence, issued, on December 6, 1810, not quite three months after he had proclaimed independence from Spain, a decree abolishing slavery in Mexico, and our first Congress, which met in Chilpancingo in 1813, issued some bases for a constitution and decreed at the same time the abolition of slavery. The abolition, of course, could only be enforced then in the few places which were occupied by the insurgents, but when independence was achieved, one of the first acts of the first Mexican Congress, convened at the City of Mexico to adopt a constitution, was to issue a decree on July 13, 1824, which abolished slavery in Mexico, and it was then actually abolished. In fact, every Mexican is born a strong anti-slavery man, so much so that we could not understand why this country should have accepted slavery and should have tried to sustain and extend it ; or why you should engage in a tremendous civil war about it, which imperilled the very existence of the United States and the great influence that they were exerting upon the destinies of mankind ; especially when the very Declaration of American Independence contains the principle that all men are born free and equal, and slavery is a contradiction of that great principle. But fortunately, slavery has been abolished here as it was in Mexico over seventy years ago, and the stain, which for so long a time tarnished the fair name of this country, has in that way been entirely obliterated.

Mr. Logan has enlightened us considerably about the advantages of the Anglo-Saxon system of jurisprudence prevailing in the United States as compared with the Roman system, which prevails in Mexico, and I confess that that subject has always had a great deal of interest for me, because, having been educated at home as a lawyer, I always desired to study and compare the various systems of jurisprudence of different countries, as one of the best ways to understand the philosophy of jurisprudence. I regret, however, that my public duties have deprived me of the opportunity to practice law at home, and hence of becoming better acquainted with all its provisions, and that the same cause has prevented me from studying the practical workings of the Anglo-Saxon system of jurisprudence as practiced in the United States.

I always thought that it would be very pleasant for me to spend a few days in visiting the courts in this country, especially in the city of New York, with a view of getting better informed as to the practical workings of your system of jurisprudence, but, unfortunately, I never had enough time at my disposal to do so. It is, therefore, with great reluctance that I approach such a difficult subject as this, as I do not believe I am fully competent to treat it as thoroughly as I would like to. Even in regard to the Mexican laws I am not so well informed as I should be if I could have practiced law at home, for, while I know the general tenor of its legislation, I have been absent many years from my country and am not so well acquainted with all its details as I would like to be. While I would not say any word derogatory of the Anglo-Saxon system of jurisprudence, I think the Roman system, being the result of several centuries of study and experience by one of the most enlightened and cultivated nations on earth, is also entitled to some regard, as is shown by the fact that the Anglo-Saxon nations are adopting some features of the Roman jurisprudence. A careful study of both would very likely lead to a conclusion in favor of an elective system, combining the best features of each.

A great deal has been said about the advantages of the Anglo-Saxon jury system, but while I am not disposed to criticise it, I will only remark that eight hundred years ago, when England was divided into different classes, and baron and commoner were struggling for the mastery each over the other, it was undoubtedly a great conquest for the rights of the people that a man should be tried by a jury of his peers. The commoners were undoubtedly oppressed both by the king and by the barons, and during the reign of King John they obtained the Magna Charta, which was then a great conquest for human rights and human liberty, and which has proved to be the corner-stone of free institutions throughout the world. The commoners realized that the best way to protect their rights and to prevent any abuse of authority by either king or baron, was to establish that they could not be arrested, except in accordance with the law of the land, or punished unless it was by a jury of their peers; but times have advanced considerably during the eight centuries which have since élapsed, and the condition of the commoner in England is not now the same as it was then, and we might say now that the barons are merging into the commoners. Certainly, so far as this country, where there are no classes, is concerned, there is no reason at all to fear that the white people will be oppressed by those in authority. The Constitution of the United States is so careful about this that it does not clothe even the President of the United States with the right to make arrests, unless it is in a very few cases specially provided by the laws, or by the treaties, as when the extradition of a fugitive from justice is required, under a treaty, by a foreign power.

For the reasons above stated, I will not express any decided convictions upon this subject, but I might say that the conditions under which the jury system was established do not prevail at the present time, even in the country of its origin, and it cannot have now the importance it once had. Its insufficiency to punish criminals is shown, I think, by its practical workings which have unfortunately often brought about what is called Lynch Law, which is really the complement of criminal proceedings under the Anglo-Saxon system. When a community is satisfied that a crime has been committed, that somebody is the author of that crime, and that the criminal cannot be punished under the regular proceedings of a common law trial, they take the law into their own hands and they administer swift justice in a way you may call barbarous, but in the only way left to them.

But the force of example, and the great credit which the Anglo-Saxon system has obtained in the world on account of its respect for human rights, has induced some of the American nations of Latin origin to adopt the jury system, and we have done so in Mexico. Señor Mariscal, our present Secretary of State, who lived in the United States from 1863 to 1877—up to 1867 as Secretary of the Legation and afterwards as Minister from Mexico in Washington—and who is a great jurist, a thorough student, and a careful observer, made a special study

of the jury system in the United States, and when he returned home
and became Secretary of Justice, he established the jury system in
Mexico for criminal cases, changing it somewhat with a view to adapting
it to the peculiar conditions of the Mexican character. He provided,
for instance, that the majority of the jurors should render a verdict,
while, under the Anglo-Saxon system, a unanimous vote of all the jurors
is required. It is the practice in Mexico that all the preliminary proceedings in a criminal case shall take place before the judge who
presides over such proceedings, without a jury, but when this is finished,
then the jury is convened and they hear the statement of the District
Attorney, the defence of the accused, and such witnesses as they desire
—both their direct testimony and their cross-examination—and finally
give their verdict, declaring the accused innocent or guilty. It is provided, besides, with a view to preventing the failure of justice, that if
in the opinion of the presiding judge the verdict is clearly against the
facts as established by the evidence, he should report to the higher
court, and if that court sustains his opinion, the verdict of the jury
should be entirely set aside and a new trial should take place. Even
with all those alterations in the truly Anglo-Saxon Jury system, I have
seen cases in Mexico in which criminals have been left unpunished
because their attorneys with their eloquence have influenced the jury in
favor of the accused. .

I do not think it is entirely correct to say that the proceedings under
the Roman law are secret and that the accused does not know what the
witnesses have said against him. This misunderstanding is sometimes
carried very far. One of the difficulties that the Spanish-American
countries have to contend with in Washington, in cases where citizens
of the United States are tried by the local judges in any of those countries, is the great difference between their legislation and criminal procedure and the system prevailing in this country. In the United States
all trials have to be public ; the accused has a right to appear in person
or to be represented by an attorney and to hear and refute all the evidence against him ; he has the right to be set at liberty on bail, whatever may be the crime imputed to him, except wilful murder : and he
has finally the right to be tried by a jury of his peers ; while in the
Spanish-American countries there prevails a legislation of Roman
origin, which may or may not be better adapted to ascertain the facts

and to do justice, but which is entirely different from the English or common law system.

In the Roman system every criminal trial is divided into two stages: the summary (*sumario*), which is secret, and the purpose of which is to find out the facts connected with the case, the testimony of the accused being taken down when he may not know who appears against him, and sometimes not even of what crime he is accused ; and the plenary (*plenario*), or second stage, in which the proceedings of the summary are made public, and all the other proceedings are public, and then the accused has the same rights as are guaranteed to him by the common law. He is allowed to go out on bail only in a very few limited cases, determined by law, and never if he is liable on conviction to bodily punishment. He is not allowed to hear the testimony against him until after the summary is over.

As my only object is to mark the principal differences between the two systems, I will refrain from saying anything about their respective advantages.

The secret proceedings of the *sumario* are very much criticised in the United States, without remembering that the English law has also a secret proceeding very similar to the *sumario*. Before anybody is indicted in this country, the case is heard secretly by a grand jury, a court composed of persons designated also secretly. The Grand Jury hears such testimony as is offered, or as they may deem sufficient, without allowing a hearing to the accused, and if there is in their judgment sufficient ground for it, the indictment is made, and after that the public trial begins before the proper court. The *sumario* corresponds, therefore, in countries of Latin origin, as far as that is possible between two legislations based on such widely different principles, to the Grand Jury indictment in the Anglo-Saxon nations. The substantial difference between the two is that under the Latin system the accused is arrested when the *sumario* begins, while in the common law system he is not arrested until after the indictment is made ; but the Latin law has provided some remedies for any possible abuse in such cases.

In the countries where the Latin system prevails, testimony is taken down in writing, read to the witness and signed by him if found correct, as a proof that he was exactly reported. There is no room, therefore, for the judge to pretend that the witness has said something different from what he really did say. When the summary is over, the whole testimony is passed over to the accused for examination, and the accused has the right to cross-examine the witnesses, if he thinks proper to do so. The cross-examination is an old Spanish proceeding which we call "careo," meaning in Spanish to confront personally the witness before the judge for the purpose of cross-examination. Therefore it is not correct to say that the accused does not know anything about the evidence taken against him, because while in the first stage he does not know it, in the second stage he has full opportunity to know all that has been said and full opportunity to refute it, either by presenting his witnesses or by cross-examining such witnesses as have been presented by the other side or called by the judge.

Some American citizens tried in Spanish-American countries expect that the proceedings will be conducted in accordance with the legislation of their own country, or some other country with a similar legislative policy, and when they find that it is not so, they complain bitterly, considering the Latin proceeding as inquisitorial, as an outrage and even barbarous ; just as if the legislation of the United States ought to be in force in those countries. My experience has shown me that this is the cause of difficulties and misunderstandings between the United States and some of the Spanish-American republics.

They complain, too, that the trial under the Roman system goes on very slowly and they aver that criminal trials in the United States come to an end more speedily. I am not prepared to say which of the two systems of criminal proceedings requires the longer time. When the trial actually begins, it may take a shorter time in the United States, because, once the trial begins, it cannot be interrupted ; but it often takes a long time before it begins, and longer when it is followed by a new or second trial. It must be borne in mind that the courts in this country hold their sessions for but a few weeks or months at a time, and only during the session do they hear cases ; while in the Latin-American countries they are open and working all the year round. Then, as a trial here takes the whole time of the court, only one case can be tried at a time, while in the Latin-American countries the judge tries several cases at the same time ; and as a consequence of this, every trial here has to be postponed until its docket number is

reached, and that sometimes requires the lapse of several months, while
in the Latin countries it begins at once.

I do not know which system of criminal jurisprudence is, on the
whole, best calculated to do justice in the establishment of the fact,
whether by a judge with long experience and proficiency in his profession and having no personal interest´ in the cases tried by him, or by a
jury of men who have no experience in criminal jurisprudence. If the
judge may sometimes be derelict in his duties, the jury occasionally are
controlled by their emotions. If the judge fails to do his duty, his
failure will be corrected by the Superior Court, as all trials have to go
to a Court of Appeals ; but for an improper verdict of a jury, there is
often no adequate remedy. The Anglo-Saxon Jurisprudence follows
the principle that it is better to leave one hundred criminals unpunished,
rather than punish one innocent person.

There is a remark in Mr. Logan's paper which needs some explana-
tion, and it refers to the summary way in which criminals are sometimes punished in Mexico. Our Constitution commences with a statement of the rights of man, taken in a great measure from the declaration of the French National Assembly during the Revolution—and this
was in a great measure taken from your Declaration of Independence—
and those rights secure the most ample liberty and immunity to the
person and property of the inhabitants of the country, as Mr. Logan
has informed us by quoting fully from that instrument. It was represented, however, while the Constitution was being discussed, that on
extraordinary occasions, as in case of war or other serious danger to
society, such rights as have been guaranteed by the Constitution, stood
very much in the way of speedy punishment. To avoid that, the Constitution itself, in its Article XXIX, provided that the rights of man, as
guaranteed by that instrument, excepting such as secure a man's life,
can be suspended for a short time, in certain emergencies, provided the
President asks Congress to suspend them and Congress agrees to do it,
and that the suspension embraces a class, and not an individual. If it
is found, for instance, that the crime of the derailing of railway cars,
either to rob them or for some other purpose, becomes frequent, and it
is thought that the emergency requires an extraordinary measure, the
President asks Congress for the suspension of the personal guarantees
of such criminals for a limited period, say six months, and if Congress

sanctions the suspension, a summary criminal proceeding is established, for the purpose of inflicting punishment without delay, and therefore frighten others who might be disposed to commit the same crime. At the end of the six months, for instance, the public confidence is restored, and there being no further need of a speedy trial, the suspension of constitutional guarantees comes to an end. It will be seen that our constitution provides a speedy way of punishing criminals in extraordinary cases, without the unfortunate need which the condition of things has made necessary sometimes in this country—especially in California in former years—of establishing a committee of public safety to preserve order, by which the people took the law in their own hands and acted without any form of law, very much as is done where Lynch Law prevails.

We have copied from you the Writ of Habeas Corpus, the great conquest of the Anglo-Saxon, which guarantees life and liberty to man, and which places under the control of the judicial courts the otherwise arbitrary orders of those in authority ; but we have gone considerably farther in that direction, and our Writ of Habeas Corpus is not limited to the protection of personal life and liberty, but extends to all the rights guaranteed to man by the Constitution—embracing his personal property—even covering judicial decisions. If a man, for instance, finds that his property, or any other constitutional rights, are interfered with by either civil or military authority, or even by a judicial sentence of a federal or State court, he applies to the respective federal district court, which has jurisdiction to suspend at once the act complained of by the plaintiff and finally to decide the case either in his favor or against him, the decision always going for revision to our Supreme Court.

So far as the Conciliation Act of which Mr. Logan spoke to us is concerned, it was intended to avoid civil suits, and for that reason the Mexican Constitution of 1824 established that before any civil suit began, the plaintiff should present a certificate that he had attempted, without avail, to settle his difficulties amicably ; but that provision was not repeated in our present constitution of 1857, and therefore it is not now in force.

To understand the condition of things in Mexico is very difficult for foreigners who are not quite familiar with the country, and even for Mexicans themselves who have not paid any special attention to this subject. The general impression of the outside world is that because Mexico has been troubled by a long series of civil wars, which lasted for over half a century, we were constitutionally disposed to fight and did so without any plausible cause or reason ; but such a view is a great mistake, and a few remarks will explain the philosophy or the real reasons of our civil wars.

During the Spanish rule in Mexico, which lasted for three centuries, there were three controlling privileged classes, the people counting for nothing at all. The first was the clergy, which, by obtaining bequests from persons who were dying, and in several other ways, had accumulated a very large fortune, owning almost two-thirds of the whole real estate of the country, and so absorbed the banking and other business. Its power depended not only upon its immense wealth, but on its religious influence and on its being the only educated class, for though it knew but little, that was a great deal more than the other classes knew, for they were kept in the most profound ignorance. Its discipline assisted the clergy in wielding great influence. The clergy had so much influence during the Spanish rule, that once a Viceroy tried to enforce his authority on a recalcitrant Archbishop of the city of Mexico by arresting him and sending him to Spain. He succeeded in making the arrest ; but the moment it was known that the Archbishop was on his way to Vera Cruz, the people rebelled in such serious manner that he was soon back in the city of Mexico, and the Viceroy had to leave.

The second privileged class were the Spaniards by birth, who formed a kind of aristocracy, some of them having titles, and who were the only ones holding office in the country, and who monopolized the principal business, and were also a rich class. This class was so jealous of the native Mexicans that even the children of a Spaniard by a Mexican mother, if born in Mexico, were not considered on the same footing as the Spaniard ; they were called creoles, had no rights at all, and could not fill any public office, nor have any position. But few Spanish women ever came to Mexico. The men came while they were young, grew up in the country, and married Mexican women, very seldom pure blooded Indians, and generally the daughters of Spaniards by Mexican mothers, born in Mexico.

The third class was the army, which was comparatively small, but was a very important element in the country, and native Mexicans were usually in very subordinate positions, and in a few cases only admitted among the commissioned officers. The opposition of the Clergy to independence and the alarm it felt at that movement were so great that the Bishop of Oaxaca, forgetting the rudimentary duties imposed upon him by his religion, organized his clergy into a regiment to fight against the insurgents, which was called the "Purples," because that was the color of the regiment's uniform— the same as the Bishop's vestments, but I understand that that martial Prelate had no occasion to come in conflict with the insurgents. The Spaniards disregarded so much the interest of their colonies, that they would not allow us in Mexico to raise the same fruits they had at home, like vine-yards and olive trees, etc., and that is the reason why we do not produce yet as much wine as we otherwise could. It was only after our independence was accomplished that we began to cultivate those fruits.

These three classes were, of course, decidedly attached to the Spanish rule, because under it they prospered and had all the wealth and power they could possibly wish, while any change might endanger their position and welfare. The only educated class was the clergy, and that was too the only profession open to native Mexicans. The higher clergy was, of course, heartily loyal to Spain, while a few members of the lower clergy, those who had some patriotic feelings, were the only ones who could appreciate the condition of things and long for a change.

Independence was proclaimed in Mexico on September 15, 1810, in an Indian village in the State of Guanajuato, by Miguel Hidalgo y Costilla, the curate of the town, and quite an old man, assisted by two inferior officers of the Mexican militia. His enterprise was bound to fail, for the leading classes of Mexico were against it. He collected a very large number of peasants and poor people, who followed his lead. To raise the public enthusiasm on his side, he had to put his cause under the protection of the Virgin of Guadalupe, who is supposed to have preternaturally appeared two hundred years before to a humble Indian, near the city of Mexico, and was highly reverenced in the country. His men were unorganized, without arms, ammunition or discipline, and although he captured some towns and made some headway, the organization and discipline of the Spanish army soon prevailed and he was defeated, captured, degraded by the higher clergy, and shot in

July, 1811.   He was succeeded by another priest, a full-blooded Indian, José Maria Morelos, who had in him the elements of a great warrior, who organized a government, convened a Congress at Chilpancingo, which issued a constitution, defeated the Spaniards in several drawn battles and sustained for several months, against great odds, the famous siege in Cuautla, near the City of Mexico, which siege was the subject of one of Mr. Logan's most interesting papers on Mexican history. Morelos fought the Spaniards from 1810 to 1815, when he was captured, degraded and shot.   After that the War of Independence was almost over.   Only a few leaders remained and those were principally in the southern part of the country where it was quite mountainous and there was a bad climate, so that it was easy to keep up the insurrection for some time, and the Spanish troops could not make much headway there.

Such was the condition of things when, in 1820, the Spaniards at Madrid restored the liberal constitution adopted by the Cortes in 1812, when King Ferdinand the VII had fled from Spain on account of the French invasion, and that fact alarmed very much the Spanish element in Mexico, who, fearing that liberal principles might find a foothold in that country, thought that the best plan for them to follow was to proclaim independence from Spain and establish a Catholic monarchy under a Spanish king, so that they would not be subject to the obnoxious changes which liberal ideas, that had begun to permeate Spain, might bring about.   They went, therefore, to Iturbide, who, although a native Mexican, had been one of the leaders of the Spanish army against the insurrection, was a good soldier and an ambitious man. Iturbide accepted their plan, and when appointed by the Viceroy to command the army sent to subdue the southern revolutionary leaders, he took all the forces and money of the Viceroy and joined Guerrero and the other revolutionary leaders.   After that independence was accomplished almost without a blow, and Iturbide was then crowned Emperor of Mexico.

And thus it was that the movement for independence which, in the other Spanish colonies, came from the higher classes, in Mexico came originally from the lower classes, with the higher classes opposing it, and thus it was that the first movement was an apparent failure.   As soon as it became for the interest of the higher classes themselves that

Mexico should be independent of Spanish rule, their influence turned the scale, and independence was achieved. The Mexican patriots who had been fighting for ten years in favor of independence, material progress, and liberal principles, could not be satisfied with the establishment of an empire. They thought that this was depriving them of the fruits of their victory, and so they rebelled against Iturbide and inaugurated a revolution which finally overthrew the empire and made Iturbide fly from the country. That renewed the old hostility between the two parties—the Liberal party, which had been the promoter of independence and desired progress, and the Conservative or Church party, which intended to maintain the *statu quo* and was decidedly averse to any changes. It is not strange that the conflict between these two parties, representing such antagonistic ideas, should have lasted so long.

After Iturbide's downfall, the Liberals summoned a national congress, which issued, on January 31, 1824, the preliminary basis of a Federal Constitution. Finally, on October 4th, of the same year, the Constitution itself, as finally promulgated, was adopted. It was patterned after the Constitution of the United States and was almost a copy of it, and I do not know whether, in imitating your institutions so closely, we did not make a mistake. The constitution of a country should be adapted to the conditions of that country. Here, in your northern country, there were thirteen independent colonies, which made war against England, achieved their independence, and then found themselves little more than a confederacy of infantile nations, with all the weaknesses which ever have attended a simple confederation. They, therefore, decided to consolidate themselves into a strong nation, under the name of "The United States of America." The federal system of government was the only solution of the problems which confronted your people then. It was the natural and inevitable outgrowth of the condition of things existing before the adoption of the constitution. In Mexico, there was a united country, subject to the same authorities and laws, and with only one head. In adopting a Republican federal system there, the nation had to be artificially divided up into separate sections, to be called States, which had no separate existence before, and no individual history or experience in self-government. It is not to be wondered at, therefore, that when this Constitution went into

operation, it caused great disturbance. It is easy to find in this condition one of the causes of our prolonged civil wars. We were not
alone in our misfortunes, for almost every other nation on this continent
followed in our footsteps and tried to adapt the republican-federal system to a condition of things to which it was not adaptable. Brazil,
alone, escaped this period of chaos and experiment by establishing an
empire, with a scion of the reigning house of Portugal on the throne, and
did not adopt a federal-republican form of government until nearly a
century later, after the·people had acquired some ideas about self-government, and some capacity for it ; and it is probably for these reasons
that she has suffered less by civil commotions than any other country
of the same origin in this hemisphere.

Our Constitution of 1824 was a decided victory for the Liberal
party, but it was very far from being a final one. The Church Party,
though then defeated, was really the stronger of the two. The Liberal
victory did not last long and the Conservative or Church Party prevailed upon some of Mexico's numerous military leaders to rebel against
the government and inaugurate a revolution which ended in 1835 in
the overthrow of the Constitution of 1824. As that party was so rich
and so strong and had so much influence in the country, it could very
easily bring about a civil war of such seriousness that it was very difficult for the Liberal side to overcome it ; but as time elapsed, the
Liberal Party, which really represented the patriotic element of the
country, grew stronger with education and contact with foreign nations
and was materially assisted in its task by the demoralization of the
clergy and their unpatriotic conduct during our foreign wars—besides
the civil wars, we had, in 1828, a war against Spain, who sent an ex-
pedition to conquer Mexico ; in 1838, a war with France ; in 1846 and
1847, war with the United States ; and from 1861 to 1867, the war of
the French Intervention. It was not difficult, therefore, for the Liberal
Party to inaugurate in their turn a counter-revolution which was at last
successful and which finally restored them to power.

It was in that way that the period of our civil wars continued so
long and that we came to have many different constitutions. While the
Church Party had the ascendency, they issued on October 23, 1835,
some bases for a constitution which was finally proclaimed on December
29, 1835, under the title of Constitutional Laws, and which abolished

the Federal system of Government and several of the Liberal features of the Federal Constitution. This constitution did not seem to be conservative enough to the Church Party, and they issued on June 13, 1843, what we called the " Organic Bases," and these are the two constitutions to which Mr. Logan referred in his paper. It happened therefore that when the Liberals were in power, a Federal Constitution was issued or the old one restored, and when the Church Party had the ascendency they proclaimed a Conservative Constitution or established a dictatorship. Finally, on May 18, 1847, the Federal Constitution of 1824, with some amendments, was restored, and the Liberal Party regained power which they kept until 1853, when Santa Ana returned to Mexico, called back by a successful revolution of the Church Party, notwithstanding that in former years he had been a leader of the Liberal Party. It was then that he established the dictatorship which Mr. Logan has described. But the Liberals rebelled against him again, proclaiming the plan of Ayutla, and in 1855 Santa Ana fled from the country. A Federal Government was then established under General Alvarez first, and General Comonfort afterwards. General Alvarez appointed Benito Juarez Secretary of Justice, and it was on November 23, 1855, that Juarez, as such Secretary, issued the first law against the clergy which deprived them of the privileges they had enjoyed before. Under the Spanish rule and also after the independence of Mexico, up to that date, the clergy had special courts made up of clergymen, to try them for any offence that they might commit. This was a privilege which insured them almost perfect immunity and exempted them from the control of the laws of the country. The Liberals thought that that was a great outrage, but they could not change the condition of things until the Juarez law was issued in 1855. The army enjoyed the same privileges, of which the Juarez law deprived them by restricting the jurisdiction of military courts to military offences only.

The Juarez law was succeeded by the Lerdo law, which provided that no corporation—meaning the clergy, as the Church was the only corporation existing in Mexico—could hold real estate, and that such as was held by any corporation should be sold to the actual tenants at a price which was to be arrived at by capitalizing the rent on the basis of six per cent. rate of interest. Thereafter, the tenant was to be the owner of the property, the corporation retaining a mortgage equal to the price fixed in this way. These two laws were the cause of another insurrection promoted by the Church, and which was subdued by President Comonfort. But unfortunately, he afterwards wavered and allowed himself to be influenced by the clergy. The Constitution of February 5th, 1857, had been issued during the administration of Comonfort and he had just taken the oath to support it, and under it had been elected Constitutional President for a term of four years. Notwithstanding this and the fact that he had successfully subdued one insurrection of the Church, he finally allowed himself to be used as the tool of the clergy, and headed a revolution against the very constitution which he had proclaimed and by virtue of which he held his power.

Juarez, after the enactment of the law which bore his name, had, for a time, been Governor of the State of Oaxaca, and, while holding that office, he had been elected Chief Justice of the Republic and *ex-officio* Vice-President, and was, at the time of the Comonfort rebellion, also acting as Secretary of the Interior.

He became Comonfort's successor and undertook to stem the tide of rebellion and reaction. In the City of Mexico, most of the old regular army of the country were in favor of the Conservative or Church Party. The City, therefore, fell into the hands of Juarez's enemies and he had to fly from it. He went to the interior where he established his government, first at Queretaro, afterwards at Guanajuato and Guadalajara. Finally he sailed from Manzanillo, a Mexican port on the Pacific, to Panama, New Orleans, and back to Vera Cruz on the Atlantic coast, where he remained for some time. Vera Cruz was the stronghold of the Liberal Party. It was naturally a strong place and well fortified. It was protected also by its bad climate and the prevalence of yellow fever there, and was the best place he could have selected to establish his government. He remained at Vera Cruz from March, 1858, to December, 1860, during which time the principal cities of the country were in the hands of the Church Party. The Liberal army, though often defeated, was never destroyed, for the people were with them and recruits came in abundance. After a defeat, they reorganized their armies and were soon ready to meet the enemy again. Their courage and persistence were finally rewarded, and they were victorious in the decisive battle of Calpulalpan on the 24th of December, 1860. During the terrible struggle which we call the War of Reform,

Juarez issued from Vera Cruz our Reform Laws, which had for their object to destroy the political power that the clergy had exercised before. The church property was declared national property and was sold by the government to the occupants of it at a nominal price, payable partially in national bonds, then selling at a very great discount. Thus was the clergy deprived of all political rights. Their convents, both of monks and nuns, were suppressed. The number of churches existing in the country was considerably reduced. Complete independence between the Church and the State was proclaimed. A civil registry of births, marriages and deaths was established, taking from the clergy all interference with such subjects which had been up to then under their sole supervision.

Processions and all other religious demonstrations outside of the church, as well as the ringing of bells, were prohibited. The number of feast days, which then amounted to nearly one-fourth of all the days of the year and tended to keep the people in idleness, was reduced to not more than two or three for the whole year. The wearing outside of the church of the priest's peculiar habit was prohibited and many other stringent measures against the Church were adopted, with a view to destroy its political power and to deprive it of the means to bring about another insurrection against the government.

It is a remarkable fact that most of the Liberal leaders were lawyers. It was lawyers, who, influenced solely by patriotism and a desire for the success of the Liberal cause and without any military education, had to lead our armies during the long civil wars. Some of them became very distinguished soldiers in our war, as in yours here in the United States. Mr. Logan is therefore correct when he says that the final success of the Liberal cause in Mexico was due in a great measure to the jurists of the nation, so much so that they incurred the special hatred of the Church party, and the name of "lawyer" was wont to be used by them as a contemptuous designation for the Liberal leaders.

After the battle of Calpulalpan, where General Miramon, the last Church Party President, was defeated, Juarez left Vera Cruz and established his government at the City of Mexico. He then convened congress, ordered an election, and in 1861 he was elected President for his first constitutional term. The Reform Laws did not become operative until after Juarez occupied the City of Mexico and his rule extended over the whole country. The Church Party did not give up the struggle, but began it again with renewed vigor and started a new insurrection in 1861 especially against the execution of the Reform Laws. This insurrection was not of a serious character, because they could not capture any important places or defeat the government troops, but they did succeed in keeping up an unsettled condition of things throughout the country.

When the Church Party became satisfied that the Liberal Party had grown so that they did not have strength enough at home to overcome it, they went to Europe and began an intrigue with European courts to secure a European intervention in Mexico. Unfortunately, about that time the civil war in the United States broke out. The French emperor seemed quite certain of the success of the Confederacy, and was very well disposed to avail himself of the opportunity offered by the Mexican Church Party of gaining a foothold in Mexico and of effectually aiding in the permanent division of the United States. He had, besides, his dreams of establishing a French empire in America bordering on the Pacific. Under his influence, an alliance was made between France, England and Spain, and Maximilian was persuaded to come to Mexico. England and Spain withdrew before the war actually began, and Napoleon's army was defeated at Puebla on the 5th of May, 1862 ; but after being considerably reinforced, he succeeded in occupying both Puebla and the City of Mexico in 1863, and so began the French Intervention. You are familiar with the details of that intervention and I will not say anything more about it. When peace was restored in this country, after the collapse of the confederacy, Napoleon, of course, understood that he could not continue for an indefinite period his occupation of Mexico, and that he had to give up his Mexican plans, and withdraw his army from the country. Maximilian well knew that he could not remain in Mexico after the withdrawal of the French, and he decided to leave the country as soon as he heard that the French army was to be withdrawn ; but unfortunately he was not a man equal to the occasion. He was not steady in his resolutions, and he was persuaded by the leaders of the Church Party to return to the City of Mexico. He had already started on his homeward journey and gone so far as Orizaba, very near Vera Cruz, where the " Novara," the same Austrian man-of-war which had brought him to Mexico in 1864, lay ready to take him back to his native country, having been sent over at his request by the Emperor of Austria. It was in March, 1867, that he returned to the City of Mexico. Shortly afterwards he went to Queretaro, where he was finally captured and shot, as you all know. In July of that year, the Juarez government was again restored to the City of Mexico, and another election took place, in which Juarez was almost unanimously elected by the people for another term from 1867 to 1871.

After the French Intervention, believing that it would be good to establish some competition to the Catholic Church in Mexico, by which she would profit herself, I sold, as Secretary of the Treasury, to a Protestant congregation, of which I was not a member, for the nominal price of $4,000 in government bonds, the finest church in Mexico, after the cathedral. It was very well situated, and I think could not be built now for $1,000,000. I have just heard that the building has been recently sold for a large amount of money and is to be opened again as a Catholic church.

In a country where civil war had lasted for such a long time everything was demoralized, and so, even after our complete success against the French Intervention and the so-called Empire of Maximilian, some uprisings took place, which were now headed by dissatisfied Liberal leaders, and although they were of no serious nature and were easily subdued by President Juarez, they kept the country in an unsettled condition and contributed to support the view that we were unable to maintain peace. President Juarez died on July 18, 1872, and President Lerdo de Tejada, who succeeded him, first as Vice-President and afterwards as constitutional President, held the office until November, 1876, when General Diaz became President. Among the many distinguished services that General Diaz has rendered to Mexico, perhaps the principal one is to have restored complete peace to the country. During the several terms during which he has filled the executive office, he has earnestly encouraged the material development of the country and firmly established peace and order. Material development always furnishes the best of security that the public peace will be maintained.

It will be readily seen by this incomplete synopsis that the causes which brought about the civil wars in Mexico are now over. Ours was a contest for supremacy between the vital forces of the nation, between the old and the new ideas, which in other countries has taken long years, and even centuries, to be settled ; but now our political problem is solved, the Church party has completely broken down as a political organization and cannot cause again any serious disturbance, and the elements of civil war are now lacking. Mexico, now for nearly twenty years, has been at peace and enjoyed all the advantages of a permanent peace. Such persons as took part in former revolutions have either died, disappeared, or are now interested in the maintenance of peace, because they are thriving under the development of the country. Even in case President Diaz's guidance should fail Mexico, I am sure that peace would be preserved, because the interests in its favor are very strong. Railways and telegraphs are great preservers of peace. In case of an insurrection, it was not long ago that it took months before the government could reach the insurgents, and in the meantime they could organize and fortify themselves and make considerable headway before they were confronted by an enemy. Now the government can send troops at once to quell it.

It is only necessary to understand the philosophy of the disturbances with which we were afflicted for over fifty years to see that the causes which produced them no longer exist. I consider, therefore, that peace in Mexico is as secure as it is in any other country, and that life and property are as safe there as anywhere else. Public opinion seems to share this view, and capital, especially foreign capital, which is so conservative and timid, is now being freely invested in Mexican enterprises.

Before finishing my conversation, I beg of you to allow me to say a few words about Juarez of whom Mr. Logan has spoken with such encomium. His career was really remarkable. He was a full-blooded Indian, born in a small town inhabited only by Indians, and where there was but one man—the parish priest—who spoke Spanish and could read and write. Juarez was so anxious to learn Spanish and to acquire an education, that he offered his services to the priest under condition that he should be taught. The priest found him so intelligent that he sent him to the city of Oaxaca to be educated. From such humble beginnings, he rose to be a prominent lawyer and a foremost statesman. He was, at different times, Secretary of State of his own state, Member of the State Legislature, State Senator, Governor of his state for several terms, Representative to the Federal Congress, Secretary of Justice and of the Interior, Chief Justice, Vice-President, and finally President of the Republic. His principal characteristics were his profound conviction of liberal principles, his very clear mind, his remarkably good common sense, his great moral courage, his unimpeached integrity and honesty, his great patriotism, his tenacity of purpose and devotion to civil government. In time of war, when the destinies of the country were in his hands and depended on the result of a battle, and when many others in his place would have led an army, he purposely abstained from exercising any military duties. These he left entirely to those of his associates who had shown talent for war, and he himself set the example of a purely civil government. He had as much personal courage as any man in the world. I saw him more than once, facing death as near and sure as any man ever did, with perfect calmness and almost indifference, but without bravado. I am sure he felt that it is best for a patriot to die in the service of his country, because in that case he wins for himself immortality, and it is on this theory that I account for the fact that he was never afraid to die if he died while in the performance of a patriotic duty. His physical courage was as great as his moral courage, and it was by no means easy for him to resist the temptation to try to win for himself some military laurels during the War of the French Intervention. He had been in this country as an exile, living for some time in New Orleans, where he supported himself by working as a cigar maker. He admired your free institutions, and it was his earnest wish to establish them in Mexico and to see everybody there as happy and free as he had seen the people of the United States.

Another of his characteristics was his tenacity of purpose and his devotion to the right. His saying that "peace is respect for the rights of others" has become an axiom among us. There was a time, during the French Intervention, in which many seemed to despair of the fate of Mexico, and that feeling was not entirely unreasonable, considering that the country was invaded by a very large French army—some sixty or eighty thousand men, I think. Besides, Napoleon and Maximilian had contrived to have an Austrian Auxiliary Corps, besides a corps from Hungary, and another from Belgium—Maximilian's wife was a daughter of the former King of Belgium and a sister of the present King—and he had also one contingent from the French colony of Algiers and the command of the troops of the Church party, which were on his side and embraced most of our old regular army, and, finally, he had all the aristocratic elements of Mexico in his favor. Altogether, the array was so great that it was no wonder that many of our public men had, sometimes, little hope of success. But Juarez never despaired for a second. He was as certain of final success as we are now that, after the great darkness of this night, the sun will rise to-morrow, to shed its brilliant light upon us and give new life to the earth. His sense of duty was so rigid that, having established his government during the French Intervention at El Paso del Norte, a small town on the right bank of the Rio Grande, where he remained for about three years, he never crossed the river to visit the opposite side, for fear that such visit might be considered as a desertion of his post.

Mr. Seward's estimate of the character of Juarez, shows how the Anglo-Saxon was impressed by the little Indian. When Mr. Seward visited Mexico on his trip around the world, he was heartily welcomed by my country and in a remarkable speech that he made in the City of Puebla, he said that Juarez was the greatest man that he had ever met in his life. His speech was taken down in shorthand and Mr. Thomas H. Nelson, of Terre Haute, Indiana, then United States Minister to Mexico, noticing this phrase and thinking that in the excitement of the moment Mr. Seward had gone further than he intended and further than he would like to have repeated after a sober second thought, took it to Mr. Seward and said to him, "Governor, will you be willing to stand by what you said in your speech, about Juarez being the greatest man you ever knew? Remember that you have been the peer and contemporary of Webster, Clay, Calhoun, and many other distinguished men of our country, and that you place Juarez above them all." Mr. Seward answered, "What I said about Juarez was after mature consideration, and I am willing to stand by my opinion." I think to quote this opinion is the best thing I could say of Juarez before an Anglo-Saxon audience.

I could enlarge this conversation, mentioning a great many other incidents about the condition of Mexico, which support the views I have presented here this evening, and I could say a great deal more about the remarkable life of President Juarez and other topics which have been touched upon in Mr. Logan's paper; but I feel that it would be intruding too much upon your valuable time. I understand that most of the ladies and gentlemen present here have other engagements for the evening which are awaiting them, and I have already spoken longer than I intended. I will, therefore, close my remarks by again thanking you very sincerely for the great honor that you have conferred upon me in inviting me to be present at this meeting and to address you to-night.